Wilf had come round to play.

"Wilma's got a netball match tomorrow, so my mum is taking me to Huntley Hall," he told Biff. "It's a stately home. Do you and Chip want to come, too?"

Biff was not sure. "Thanks, Wilf. But stately homes aren't very exciting, are they?"

"This one is!" said Wilf.

He pulled out a book from his bag. It was all about ghosts.

Huntley Hall

"Look," he said, turning to the right page.
"It says here that once, a long time ago, someone
actually saw ghosts at Huntley Hall!" Wilf
grinned. "What if *we* saw a ghost there?"

Just then Chip came into the room.

"What's that about ghosts?" he said.

"Wilf thinks there might be ghosts at Huntley Hall," explained Biff. "But there are no such things as ghosts, are there?"

Chip thought about this. "I don't *think* so,"
he said.

Just then, he noticed a familiar light in
the corner. The magic key was glowing.

"I hope this doesn't mean we're going
somewhere spooky," said Chip.

The magic took the children to the grounds of a big house at night.

"This place looks a *bit* spooky," said Chip.

"It's Huntley Hall!" said Wilf. "I recognize it from the picture."

"It's cold and windy out here," said Biff.
"Should we see if anyone is in?"

Before she could knock on the front door, Wilf
gave it a gentle push.

"It's open," he said. "Let's have a look around."

It was dark and quiet inside the house.

"Actually this place is *very* spooky," whispered Chip.

"Maybe that's why we're here," said Wilf. "So we can see the ghosts of Huntley Hall!"

"There are no such things as ghosts," said Biff
quietly. "I'm sure that . . ." She stopped. "Hold on.
What's that noise?"

A soft scratching sound was coming from
behind a closed door.

"What do you think is making that noise?"
whispered Chip.

Biff held one finger to her lips as she went to
the door. She reached for the handle and slowly
turned it.

The children stepped into a large room lit
by oil lamps.

There was a piece of paper on the table and
a chair was pulled out, but there was no sign
of anybody.

Chip picked up the paper on the table.

"It's a drawing of those flowers over there," he said. "But who made it?"

"I know!" said Wilf. "A ghost must have done it! The ghost of Huntley Hall!"

The children jumped when a voice said,
"I am *not* a ghost!"

A boy stood up from a hiding place behind
the desk.

"*I* was sketching those flowers," he said.

The boy said his name was Henry.

"Why were you hiding behind the desk?"
asked Biff.

"I heard a noise in the hall and got worried,"
Henry explained.

"I want to be an artist," he went on. "But my
father thinks that's silly. He gets cross when I
sketch. So I wait until everybody is asleep."

"You're a good artist, too," said Chip.

"I've got an idea," said Biff. "Why don't you
sketch the three of us?"

Henry smiled. "That would be nice," he said.

Wilf put his hands on his hips and stuck his
chin out. "How's this?" he joked.

Henry pointed to the fireplace.

"Perhaps you should just all stand over there,"
he said.

He took a fresh piece of paper and began to
sketch. Biff, Chip and Wilf concentrated hard on
not moving a muscle.

Suddenly a gust of wind blew through the open window. The curtains billowed and knocked one of the lamps over.

It fell onto a scrunched-up piece of paper.

"It's on fire!" cried Henry in alarm.

The other children turned to see the flame catch at the bottom of the long curtain. There was no way to put the fire out. It climbed quickly, growing bigger and bigger.

"Quick!" said Biff. "We have to wake everybody in the house up!"

The children ran to the hall and began to shout, "Wake up! Fire!" at the top of their voices.

They heard footsteps clumping, and then a big
man in a nightshirt raced down the stairs.

"Where's the fire? What's going on, Henry?"
he demanded.

Henry pointed through the open door to
the study.

Henry's father took a deep breath. Then he shouted in a booming voice, "Servants! We need water in the study right now!"

The children could hear more footsteps and shouts all around the house.

Moments later several servants appeared.
They were carrying buckets, pans and anything
else that would hold water.

When they threw the water onto the fire, it
let out an angry-sounding hiss.

At last the fire was out.

"Who left a window open and an oil lamp lit?" asked Henry's father with a scowl.

"I believe you did, dear," said Henry's mother from the stairs.

It was only then that Henry's father noticed Biff, Chip and Wilf.

"Who are you three?" he demanded. "What are you doing here?"

Luckily the magic key had begun to glow in Biff's pocket.

Before they disappeared, Chip just had chance to give Henry a final word of advice. "Don't give up art! You're really good!"

The last thing they saw was Henry smiling.

The next instant the three children were back
in Biff's bedroom.

"It's a pity we didn't see any ghosts," said Wilf.

They all agreed that it had been an exciting
adventure anyway.

The next day Biff and Chip went with Wilf
and his mum to Huntley Hall.

Wilf's mum was happy to see how interested
the three children were in the Hall's history.

The tour guide led them into the study.

"Two hundred years ago, a fire started in this room," the guide said. "It might have destroyed the house, but three mysterious strangers warned the Huntley family just in time."

"Nobody knew who they were, but it was lucky they were there," continued the guide. "Then they just vanished."

The children looked at each other in surprise.

"We didn't meet any ghosts," whispered Wilf. "I think we *were* the ghosts!"

In the next room, the tour guide talked about people who had lived in the house.

"Henry Huntley became a successful artist," she said. "Here's Henry's painting of his father, who claimed to be his biggest fan."

There were several of Henry's paintings and sketches in the room.

"Look at this one," said Wilf's mum. "It looks a bit like you three!"

The children just smiled, remembering the night when Henry drew their picture.